MEDICAL DETECTING

DETECTING
HEART DISEASE

by Rachel Kehoe

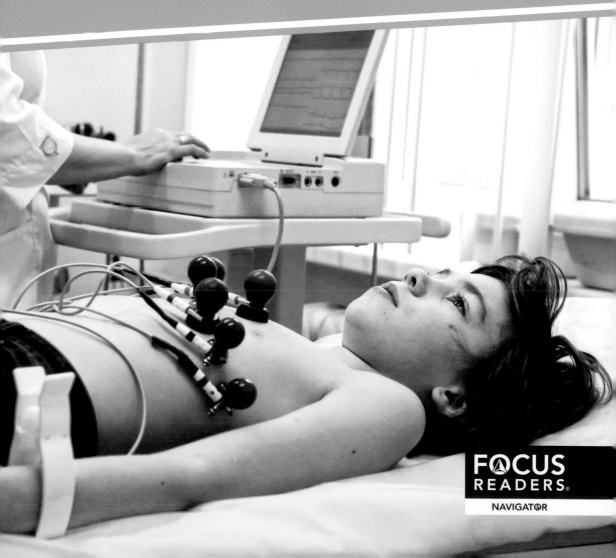

FOCUS
READERS®
NAVIGATOR

WWW.FOCUSREADERS.COM

Focus Readers is distributed by North Star Editions:
sales@northstareditions.com | 888-417-0195

Produced for Focus Readers by Red Line Editorial.

Content Consultant: Zahra Keshavarz-Motamed, PhD, Professor of Biomedical Engineering and Mechanical Engineering, McMaster University, Canada

Photographs ©: Shutterstock Images, cover, 1, 4–5, 6, 8–9; iStockphoto, 10, 12–13, 14, 16, 18–19, 20, 22, 25, 26–27, 28

Library of Congress Cataloging-in-Publication Data
Names: Kehoe, Rachel, author.
Title: Detecting heart disease / by Rachel Kehoe.
Description: Lake Elmo, MN : Focus Readers, [2024] | Series: Medical
  detecting | Includes bibliographical references and index. | Audience:
  Grades 4-6
Identifiers: LCCN 2022059430 (print) | LCCN 2022059431 (ebook) | ISBN
  9781637396254 (hardcover) | ISBN 9781637396827 (paperback) | ISBN
  9781637397916 (pdf) | ISBN 9781637397398 (ebook)
Subjects: LCSH: Heart--Diseases--Diagnosis--Juvenile literature.
Classification: LCC RC683 .K44 2024 (print) | LCC RC683 (ebook) | DDC
  616.1/2075--dc23/eng/20221223
LC record available at https://lccn.loc.gov/2022059430
LC ebook record available at https://lccn.loc.gov/2022059431

Printed in the United States of America
Mankato, MN
082023

ABOUT THE AUTHOR

Rachel Kehoe is a science writer and children's author. She has published several books and articles on science, technology, and climate change. Rachel is interested in research about nutrition and how food impacts health. She calls Ontario, Canada, her home.

TABLE OF CONTENTS

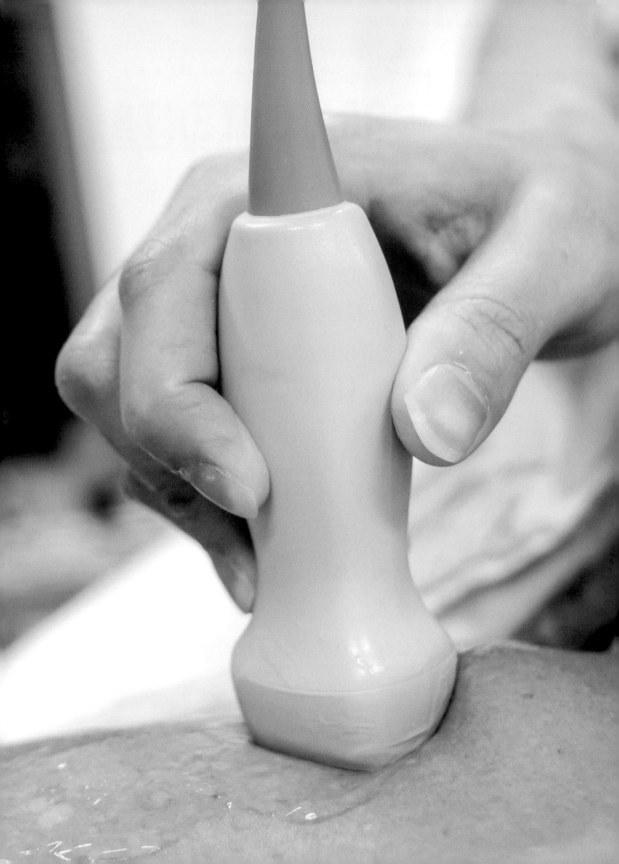

CHAPTER 1

EXAMINING THE HEART

A patient lies down on an exam bed. He is having an **echocardiogram**. The operator tells him to stay still. She puts a gel on his chest. Next, she places a machine on the gel. She presses it against the patient's skin. The machine makes sound waves. They bounce off different parts of the patient's heart.

The gel used in an echocardiogram helps the device connect closely to the patient's skin.

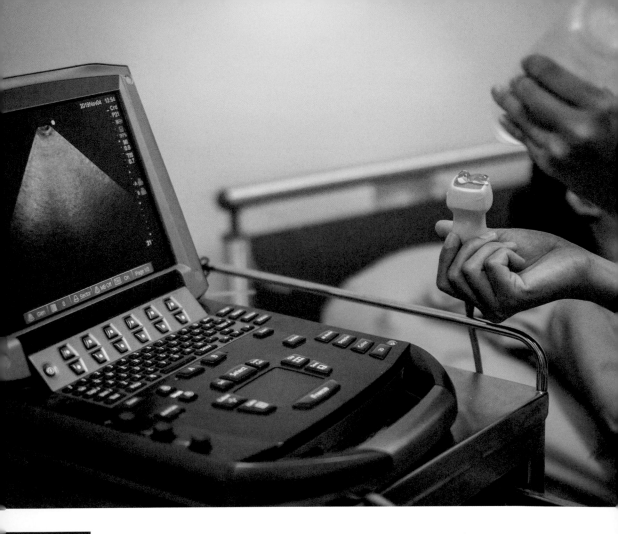

The piece that gets gel and goes on the patient's body is called the transducer.

Then, the waves "echo" back to the machine. The machine can use the waves to make pictures of the heart. The doctor can see those pictures on a screen.

During the test, the patient hears loud sounds. The noise comes from blood flowing through his heart. His **valves** open and close. They let blood flow from one area of the heart to another. Then blood goes around the body.

Hearts need good blood flow to work correctly. But sometimes diseases limit blood flow. If the patient has a heart problem, the echocardiogram can help detect it. It is one tool doctors can use to **diagnose** heart disease.

The operator finishes the test. She says the patient can go. A doctor will study the images of his heart. Then she will tell him the results.

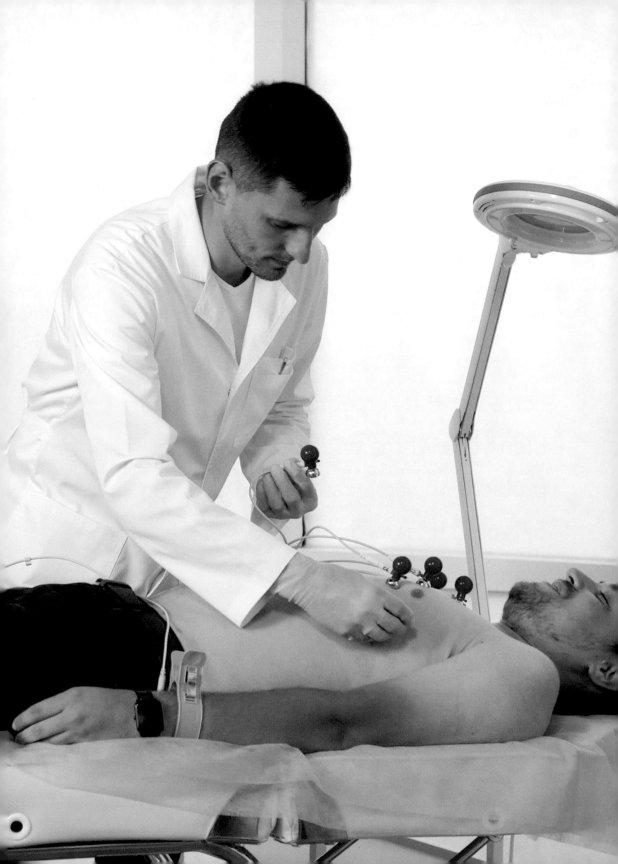

CHAPTER 2

EARLY DETECTION

Before the 1900s, doctors had little idea what happened in the heart. Then, in 1902, a Dutch doctor invented the electrocardiogram (ECG). It could record the heart's electrical activity. Doctors could use it to listen to the heart's blood flow. They could study problems such as chest pain.

During an ECG, pieces called electrodes are placed on a patient's body. They help send information.

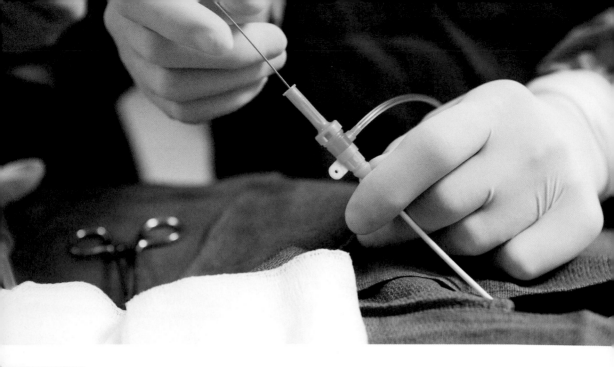

The tubes that enter the body in cardiac catheterization are made of plastic.

In 1929, a German doctor first used cardiac catheterization. That's when a **catheter** goes into the body. Then it is gently moved toward the heart. Doctors can see inside the heart's arteries. The device helps doctors find problems like **plaque** buildup. That can slow down blood flow.

Two new tests were developed in the 1950s. Echocardiograms make images of the heart. In angiograms, doctors put dye into patients' blood. The dye shows up on X-rays. Doctors can see blocked blood vessels. These tests made diagnosing heart disease possible.

KINDS OF HEART DISEASE

Sometimes people are born with heart disease. That is called congenital heart disease. But sometimes people get heart disease as adults. High blood pressure, smoking, and unhealthy diets can cause it. The most common heart disease is coronary artery disease. Plaque builds up in arteries. It can cause heart attacks. Heart attacks happen when blood can't flow to the heart.

CHAPTER 3

DIAGNOSING HEART DISEASE

Each year, one in five deaths in the United States is caused by heart disease. Many people have no **symptoms**. That's why early detection is important. Screening tests can reveal blockages. Doctors still use older tools to detect heart disease. They use newer methods like CT and MRI scans, too.

Regular checkups with doctors can help people keep up with heart health.

To detect heart disease, doctors first review patients' medical histories. They can look at chest X-rays and blood tests. After studying the results, a doctor may

HOW THE HEART PUMPS BLOOD

The heart pumps blood through different areas of the heart and around the whole body.

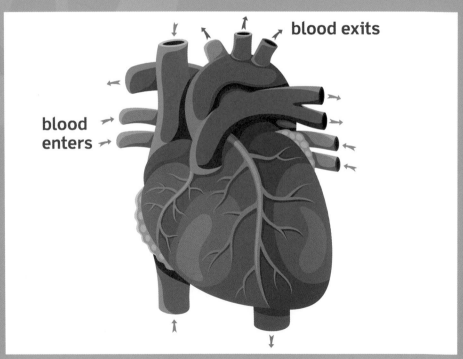

blood exits

blood enters

order a CT scan. First, the patient lies on a bed. Sometimes dye is put into the blood. Then the bed slides into a large tube. It shoots X-rays through the body. That creates a picture. Many images are stacked to make a 3D model. Plaque buildup shows up in white on scans. In this way, CT scans can give information about narrowed arteries.

Another modern detection method is a heart MRI scan. MRI machines use magnets and radio waves. They create detailed pictures of the heart, too. The images highlight plaque buildup. MRI scans can even reveal plaque inside artery walls.

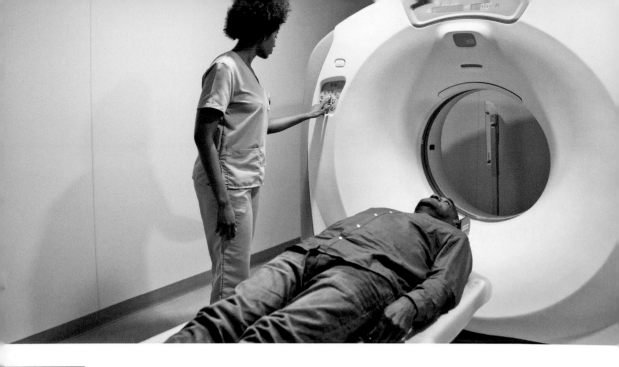

Sometimes patients must avoid solid foods for a few hours before CT scans.

Doctors can also use devices with tiny **probes** to detect heart disease. First, doctors make a cut. Then probes move into the arteries of the heart. They let cameras or other technology through. That helps show images of the artery walls. Probe tests are sensitive. They can detect early-stage heart disease.

Doctors may also use blood tests to determine heart damage. When the heart is stressed, it releases certain proteins. High levels of those proteins can signal a problem. Doctors use this test to measure the risk of heart attack.

LOWERING THE RISK

Healthy lifestyle habits can reduce the risk of heart disease. Doctors recommend that people eat many fruits and vegetables. They suggest avoiding fried foods. Regular exercise, like a daily 30-minute walk, is also important. People should also avoid smoking. Chemicals in tobacco harm the heart and blood vessels. Doctors recommend getting enough sleep, too. These healthy choices work together to protect the heart.

CHAPTER 4

ADVANTAGES AND DISADVANTAGES

Detection tests have many benefits. Several tests can observe the heart from outside the body. Those tests include ECGs, chest X-rays, and CT scans. Since they happen outside the body, patients don't need to be cut open. So, the tests don't cause bleeding. They reduce the risk of infection. They are

Modern technologies like CT and MRI scans give detailed information to doctors.

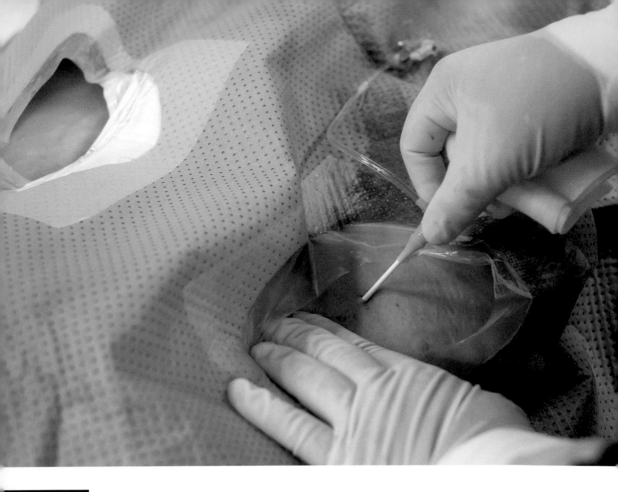

Cardiac catheterization involves outside objects entering a patient's body.

quick and painless, too. But some of these tests are not sensitive enough. They could miss hidden problems.

Invasive tests are more sensitive. Cardiac catheterization is one example.

Doctors can view the heart and arteries from inside the body. That is because they cut into a patient's skin. An instrument is placed inside. Invasive tests are very accurate. But they can cause bleeding and bruising. An infection may appear. Sometimes problems from procedures can cause blocked brain arteries. That could lead to serious problems such as strokes.

MRI scans are very useful. They don't have many drawbacks. But MRI machines use strong magnets. That means MRI machines can't be used for patients with metal in their bodies. If the magnets pulled metal into the machine, patients

Doctors called radiologists work with tests that make images of the inside of the body.

could be hurt. Doctors and patients have to consider the risks before doing these tests.

Radiation is another downside of some methods. CT scans make detailed images of the heart. But they use radiation.

Over time, radiation increases the risk of cancer. So, doctors try to avoid using too much. However, scans without radiation cost more. They also take more time. Doctors have to balance the benefits and problems. No test is perfect.

DIAGNOSIS AND GENDER

Heart disease is a leading cause of death for both men and women. However, it is more difficult to diagnose in women. It is harder to detect symptoms. Women also have different heart attack symptoms. They may experience nausea, sweating, or back pain. Not all patients and doctors connect those symptoms to heart attacks. So, some women might not be diagnosed. That makes heart attacks more likely.

ARTIFICIAL INTELLIGENCE

Many doctors are using artificial intelligence (AI) to diagnose heart disease. AI means a computer can make decisions on its own. AI works by studying data. It finds patterns. Then it uses that information to answer questions.

Some AI can spot different types of diseases. At a hospital in California, AI reads heart scans. The AI trained by viewing thousands of old scans. It learned from these images. Now, the AI sorts through new data. It notices heart problems. This tool can spot disease in its early stages. It helps doctors detect hidden heart disease.

AI also can read other data related to heart health. For example, it can measure fatty buildup in the arteries. It can locate damaged arteries.

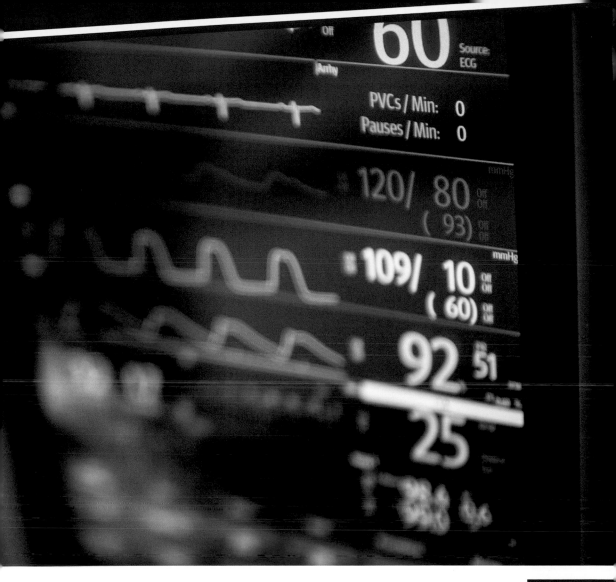

Off **60** Source: ECG

Arrhy

PVCs / Min: 0
Pauses / Min: 0

mmHg

120/ 80 Off
Off
(93) Off
Off

mmHg

109/ 10 Off
Off
(60) On
On

92 51

25

AI can use all kinds of data, such as information about heart rates, to help analyze heart health.

It can analyze blood. The AI gathers all the data. Then, it can see which patients are at risk of a heart attack. Patients can get better treatment.

CHAPTER 5

FUTURE DETECTION

Doctors and scientists are working on many new technologies. In the future, they hope to detect heart disease even earlier.

In 2017, doctors in the United Kingdom began using HeartFlow Analysis. It makes personalized images of a patient's heart. The technology focuses on blockages.

New technologies can help doctors give the best advice and treatment to their patients.

In the future, everyday technology like phones could help detect diseases.

It predicts how blockages affect blood flow. Then doctors can decide what treatment is best. HeartFlow Analysis can help patients avoid invasive procedures. Doctors might not need to use radiation.

In the future, even selfies could help predict heart disease. Some facial features are linked to heart problems.

Cloudy eyes, thinning hair, and wrinkles could be early signs. A new tool uses facial data to look for signs. It takes four photos. Each one is from a different angle. This tool could identify people who are at risk. All these new technologies could help people lead longer, healthier lives.

USING VOICES

Human voices can show signs of heart disease. Every voice has different features. Some have higher pitches. Others have nasal sounds. In 2022, researchers collected hundreds of voices. They found a pattern. Those with specific characteristics had clogged arteries. The researchers built an app. It gathered and analyzed more voices. The app correctly identified people at risk of heart disease.

FOCUS ON
DETECTING HEART DISEASE

Write your answers on a separate piece of paper.

1. Write a paragraph that describes the main ideas of Chapter 2.

2. Do you think the benefits of invasive tests outweigh the risks? Why or why not?

3. What is the most common type of heart disease?

    A. chest pain
    B. coronary artery disease
    C. heart attack

4. What could happen if plaque narrows a person's arteries?

    A. The chance of a heart attack could increase.
    B. The chance of a heart attack could decrease.
    C. The chance of a heart attack could stay the same.

Answer key on page 32.

GLOSSARY

catheter
A tube that goes into the body.

diagnose
To identify an illness or disease.

echocardiogram
A medical procedure that uses sound waves to create an image of the heart.

invasive
Involves entering the body by cutting or poking.

plaque
A fatty substance that can build up in the artery walls.

probes
Small objects inserted into patients' bodies during medical procedures.

radiation
Energy in the form of waves or particles.

symptoms
Signs of an illness or disease.

valves
Parts of the heart that control the one-way flow of blood to and from the heart.

TO LEARN MORE

BOOKS

Hulick, Kathryn. *Medical Robots*. Minneapolis: Abdo Publishing, 2019.

Silverman, Buffy. *Cutting-Edge Medicine*. Minneapolis: Lerner Publications, 2020.

Terrell, Brandon, and Dante Ginevra. *The First Heart Transplant: A Graphic History*. Minneapolis: Lerner Publications, 2022.

NOTE TO EDUCATORS

Visit www.focusreaders.com to find lesson plans, activities, links, and other resources related to this title.

INDEX

Answer Key: 1. Answers will vary; **2.** Answers will vary; **3.** B; **4.** A

MEDICAL DETECTING

Modern technology offers more ways than ever to find and diagnose problems in the body. This series highlights some of these groundbreaking innovations and inventions, as well as the science behind them.

BOOKS IN THIS SET

DETECTING BRAIN DISORDERS

DETECTING HEART DISEASE

DETECTING CANCER

DETECTING INFECTIOUS DISEASE

DETECTING CHRONIC DISEASE

DETECTING INJURY

Focus Readers deliver captivating topics, accessible text, and vibrant visuals to build reading confidence and motivate young readers.

NOTE TO EDUCATORS
Visit **www.focusreaders.com** to find:
- Lesson plans
- Activities
- Links
- Other resources related to this title

ISBN: 978-1-63739-682-7

9 781637 396827

NAVIGATOR
RL: 3–5. IL: 4–7.